PRAYERS

Kristian Doyle was born in Liverpool and lives in Paris.

ISBN: 978-1-915079-76-3

Cover designed by Aaron Kent

Edited & Typeset by Aaron Kent

Broken Sleep Books Ltd   Broken Sleep Books Ltd
Rhydwen   Fair View
Talgarreg   St Georges Road
Ceredigion   Cornwall
SA44 4HB   PL26 7YH

Prayers

Kristian Doyle

That we will believe *again* rather than *still*.

That we would be capable of answering with a single word.

That our lacks would always lack us.

That our mother would appear in a dream not shadowy, or hidden, but wholly there, addressing us.

That the plant we cut from her plant would grow more quickly.

That we will, as a way to stop thinking, become mystics.

That we will not become mystics.

That we would fuss with the Gordian knot rather than cut it.

That the falling light outside will not fall in us.

That the second-hand could stick.

That set dressers would not fill drawers whose insides the audience cannot see.

That the conditions will never be *just right*.

That we will not ask for yet another voice, in case it proliferates.

That the industrial bakery with its scent would be closer.

That Montaigne would at least once mention his mother.

That the asymmetry of others' faces in mirrors would not be metaphysically jarring.

That we will discard anything with more than one unintentional hole in.

That it would be possible to say *No, I have not read Wittgenstein*.

That we will hear tick-tock for what it really is: tick-tick.

That fewer things will be glossy.

That we will not feel thirsty merely because we don't have a drink.

That we will laugh less ostentatiously when we don't understand the joke.

That someone would say *Take a lot: take two.*

That the finished would not always be inferior to the un-.

That night thought would weigh the same as morning thought.

That the rest of the orchestra will always be busy with its own playing.

That when someone hasn't heard what we've said and asks us to repeat it we'll repeat it without changing a word.

That Hamlet's best audience would not be himself.

That we will know the date, as a matter of course.

That not using our faults will not cause us to forget we have them.

That diaristic writing would not always be working secretly on behalf of the past.

That people would *believe it* when thanked.

That we could answer any question to which we knew the answer.

That we will scratch *nothing*.

That churches would not have *For Sale* signs on them.

That we could find a useable synonym for *hello*.

That we will not cry about someone's predicament in front of the person whose predicament it is.

That we will crouch in the kitchen to look at the snail's moonlit tracks.

That peace would not depend entirely on the ability to suffer well.

That our inherited aneurysm won't rupture.

That our grandmother will think of her daughter hardly ever.

That *psyche* will again be a translation of *soul*.

That ceilings will continue, when stared at long enough, to appear to be their own rooms.

That we will not feel guilty turning plants around when they grow lopsidedly towards the sun.

That the orange candle we bought when we moved out will always have that sharp reminding holiday stink.

That we will never fall below nine and a half stone.

That we will not be the compass of our own seas.

That we will say words now and again merely for their sound, but not in public.

That we will not suffer any more epiphanies.

That every reading would not be a first reading.

That we could love someone without pitying their childhood.

That the present would not fill out only in remembrance.

That the blue sky will continue to demand new descriptions for itself.

That the world would not begin talking only after we're in the hallway, coat on.

That our happiness for others' happiness would last longer.

That we will wish people Merry Christmas first.

That gallery and museum visitors would not walk with that strange obsequious stoop.

That flirting would continue to be the basis of friendship.

That we will be pitied only when trying to be pitiful.

That we could always see the difference between refining and blunting.

That we will be wary of *grains of sand*.

That churches will not echo so loudly.

That we will no longer look down on everyone else's grieving because of our own particular experience of loss.

That we will actually *believe* in the legitimacy of other forms of grieving, rather than merely saying so.

That if our aneurysm does rupture we, like our still young mother, will die instantly.

That there will not always be someone somewhere something.

That less will be less.

That more will be more.

That enough will be *enough*.

That we will stop checking the door is locked.

That we will stop checking the oven is off.

That we will not, every night before sleep, find and then touch our keys.

That we will not, every night before sleep, turn the floor lamp away from us in case it falls in the night.

That we will let go of the idea that things often fall of their own accord in the night.

That all neighbours would not ultimately be eerie.

That no one upon receiving a gift would say to the giver the name of the gift.

That we will stop highlighting lines in books as a way of deferring properly reading them.

That ephemerality will not always add value.

That we will make it to at least forty-five. No: fifty.

That we will not use melodramatic phrases like *make it to*.

That someone will say *cold green summer night*.

That we will stop pausing films in order to comment.

That we could dismiss our own opinions as we would the opinions of others.

That snow will continue to make cushions of itself.

That we would stop asking about etiquette.

That we will buy a warm coat – one we can get several winters out of.

That drivers will continue to splash passersby.

That *the worst fog in years* will come at least yearly.

That the memories we have of our mother will slow in their dimming.

That we would feel *something* without thinking about it.

That someone would say *In ten years, these shoes won't owe you a penny*.

That we will take the night walks we've always thought about.

That we will not take the night walks we've always thought about, in case they're nothing like the night walks we've always thought about.

That nostalgia would not be the tastiest form of ingratitude.

That Weil would not envy the Crucifixion.

That we will stop seeing time as a unit of investment.

That we will no longer look into every high-ceilinged room we pass in the street.

That smoking chimneys in foreign cities will never be our interlocutors.

That we will no longer need repotting.

That we will still know the sound of our mother's voice.

That we will still be able to mimic our mother's voice.

That we will still remember her verbal expressions.

That we will still remember her physical expressions.

That warped windowglass would still craze the routes of planes.

That underlighting will be far more discriminating.

That more people will eat chocolate in public.

That old men will still open newspapers by blowing sceptically on them.

That everything in the area we grew up in would not be remembered as then-new.

That Sunday-evening will remain a feeling, but one barely remembered.

That we will not at night look up statistics on aneurysm rupture.

That we would not make the mistake in prayer of addressing anyone other than ourselves.

That we will forget the violence of the red filling the bag at the foot of her hospital bed.

That we will forget the unsouled void of her pupils seen accidentally.

That we will not repeat to ourselves the phrase *brain-stem dead*.

That we will find our own words for god.

That we will not find our own words for god.

That we will see oranges on trees hanging like hot coals in twilight.

That we will not believe filmic representations of occasions to be anything like such occasions in reality.

That we will *let* clouds form shapes.

That we would continue to lack the intelligence to see the world truly.

That we will leave five minutes earlier.

That we will remember which things are ours to tell, and which aren't.

That Coleridge would not see the sea.

That all art would be the natural history of its creator's enthusiasms.

That everyone would have objective knowledge of the smell of their own breath.

That we could account for the strength of the words *late summer*.

That we will not remember so readily that the Latin root of *intelligence* means *to choose between*.

That by touch we will know again wet morning grass.

That in passport photographs everyone would always look calmly imprisoned.

That reliving would not *always* be more living than living.

That we would throw out birthday cards.

That real houses would give us the same sensation as theme-park houses that inside faithfully resembled real houses.

That we could remember going to a pantomime.

That everyone's secrets would be the same, roughly.

That there would be no such thing as a *neutral accent*.

That we will answer the door.

That physical pain could be remembered.

That we could look at stems for as long as we look at leaves.

That the soloist would not be able to emerge only after participation in the group dance.

That calm would not only ever be a crushed calm.

That hope would not be a *response*.

That there would be a law against parents and children wearing matching outfits.

That people would more often talk with their hands, though not politicianly.

That skylines would continue in their oldfashioned camaraderie.

That we will not consider pale fingernails to be a symptom of a life-threatening disease.

That we will not consider ridged fingernails to be a symptom of a life-threatening disease.

That we will not consider hot ears to be a symptom of a life-threatening disease.

That we'll let others take the piss out of us without spoiling it by taking the piss out of ourselves first.

That trains would *never* be early.

That we could ask the old men shuffling along the promenade in their hats *What did you do with it all?*

That we'll hear more often in speech the singer.

That we would be able to feel *the feel of not to feel it*.

That we could pretend brain damage would be a pleasantly hungover train-ride home: warmly drained in the warm of the carriage, watching not completely passively the passing landscape, all questioners silent.

That the day moon, full over pine trees, would continue to mean *the rest*.

That seabirds would not look so piercingly at us – at least not when they're alone.

That *we* would be the one to step from the path to the grass, but not without thinking.

That the right comeback would not come belatedly.

That the right comeback would come *only* belatedly.

That perspicacity would not always smuggle in cruelty.

That more art would make us think we've had a hand in its making.

That someone will say *figments of the night*.

That our minds wouldn't wait till just before sleep to remind us of time.

That our minds *would* wait till just before sleep to remind us of time.

That all assimilated wisdom will not eventually look hackneyed, even daft.

That someday soon we will feel that we've been here a while.

That our mother would not've pitied us.

That in an imagined country garden, evening but the air still light, we will see a table on which a round electric lamp shines.

That belief in the existence of others really would be love.

That at every climax we won't think *If our aneurysm bursts now: fine.*

That it will all slowly, slowly disentangle itself from us.

That we'll never really feel this disentangling.

That we will remember how we once longed for the freedom we now (could) have.

That the past will not become other people.

That we will see night streets only ever by night's blues.

That there would be no such thing as off-limits.

That we would not be so naive as to think there could be no such thing as off-limits.

That plants will still be there when the light's turned on.

That birds would sing in snow.

That clothes on doors will once again turn human in the night.

That no one when quoting will do the accent.

That when we take off our clothes just before sleeping with someone, we'll remember exactly where we put them, especially in winter.

That water will be the water we walk beside, not the water we once read of.

That city moonlight would like country moonlight photograph everything in black-and-white.

That the question *Where to begin?* would soon lose some of its force.

That we would remember seeing from a train window the traintracks molten in their joining.

That we will not confuse, especially in ourselves, weakness with tenderness.

That we will be seasoned, not kiln-dried.

That animals will never be named after people. (Especially not famous people.)

That if unsure we will mark rather than not.

That time would be allowed to have its way with more of our materials.

That the ages of people we went to school with would not surprise us.

That it would be possible to talk about architecture without sounding aloofly stupid.

That it would be illegal to build houses with such small windows. (If birds don't alight on the chimney, we don't see a thing.)

That we will become far less aware of physical sensations in the head.

That we will remember that our mother won't ever be in a hospice.

That nature would not almost always mean *not-people*.

That the memory of our mother would continue (mostly) to omit her being in hospital.

That people will not talk about their children as though they're universally known.

That we will not become amateurs of our own amateurism.

That slogans on placards would continue to be misspelt.

That the extent to which people are more interesting than fictional characters would be more immediately obvious.

That we could just leave cobwebs alone.

That heavy wind rushing across sand wouldn't make a cartoon of time.

That the grey music of edge-of-sleep thought would be available to us between 10 a.m. and midday, at least twice a week.

That we can know what is and is not amenable to artefacting.

That it will not always be called *Not Yet*.

That we could play pool like silent-film comedians.

That the second half of the bottle will be better than the first, but not only because we've become used to the taste.

That handrails wouldn't retain the wet heat of others' hands.

That prayers would have less to do with the agent.

That we would not imagine doing or seeing things while doing or seeing those very things.

That if our aneurysm ruptures and we live, we'll be given a flame to watch, or a sea.

That we would never again see our mother's handwriting.

That staircases, even when walked at their edges, will creak.

That days would begin empty, end full, rather than the other way around.

That we would've spoken sooner as a child.

That rain would not be our call to leave the house.

That the horseshoe will still work even if we don't believe in it.

That our hair will never singe upward from the root.

That lying would not become even easier.

That the people who'd *never dream of telling anyone* would tell us.

That we will not pity so lavishly.

That we will never be so arrogant as to hate ourselves.

That jokes about the dead would not for us be the surest way of reifying them.

That desires would not so easily give the game away.

That the few things for which new names always occurred will go on being renamed.

That pleasure really would make us objective.

That we will not make the move to paper plates full time.

That we would never teach geography to the carrier pigeon.

That we will not, when welling up at something someone's telling us, say (proudly) *I'm welling up*.

That at parties we will avoid sober people.

That gales would blow through every other room in the dreamt house on the beach.

That we could get things down us without a strong dose of banality.

That famous people would more often have visible stains on their clothing.

That clouds when at their best would not move so quickly.

That each great artwork would be surrounded by a dozen forgettable works from the same period, so as to be like Hamlet in *Hamlet*.

That when asked what our favourite colour is we'll just play along.

That Fillan, patron saint of the mentally ill, would find some way to read other than by the light of his broken arm.

That the normal response to entrepreneurial children would be terror.

That Woolf will not hear the birds speaking Greek outside her window.

That the fellow climbers at least would be roped.

That we will not have a single *lost vehemence*.

That all art will be made with the sort of jokes you find in hymns.

That we'd remember Horatio's all-purpose reply: *So we have heard, and do in part believe…*

That everyone will be crazed with a desire to impart something they think only they know (but would not necessarily impart it).

That old actors would not perform so strenuously with their nostrils.

That we would prefer in everything Gothic cathedrals to Greek temples.

That the phrase *hotbeds of vice* would return but never unironically.

That we will not get sidetracked holding up a mirror to the mirror held up to nature.

That the best way to remember something would not be to imagine it as part of a told story.

That we will continue to see those sparks flashing up from the train's underside in darkness and snow.

That we would know what a *passage* is in painting.

That Hamlet would not be self-fathered.

That *only in art* would everything be subservient to the zodiac of the artist's wit.

That long friendship would be more than the periodic repetition of in-jokes.

That we would not blush whenever unexpectedly seeing someone we know in the street.

That there would be a greater number of parks here in which the elderly could photosynthesise.

That awnings will continue to drip long after the rain has stopped.

That when sleeping with someone we would think of no one but the person whom we're sleeping with.

That our pupils, every time we check them, will be the same size.

That we will check our pupils only twice a day.

That forgetting would not be by far the best way of bearing the past.

The hospital lights would not be shadowless.

That *haemorrhage* would be spelled differently, without that coldly archaic *ae*, that double *r* on which we still choke.

That second-hand books would not contain *Happy birthday Mum!* inscriptions.

That red skies would not on screens look so fake.

That we would not be able to see ourselves on CCTV.

That men would be given lessons in umbrellaship.

That Beckett will appear again in the same dream – the one in which he wore an off-white velour tracksuit and had two pairs of sunglasses, which he switched according to the tone he took with us.

That when someone *draws a line in the sand* we'll think only of the sand, and what'll very soon come to it.

That even the nuns would go swimming.

That sea-clothes would be left to dry in the sun.

That we will think often about returning to the great city but will never actually return.

That we won't be so ridiculous as to miss, now that we can't lift heavy objects, the strain of lifting heavy objects.

That we would not always feel safer talking than not.

That we will remember seeing the slanting rain intermittently illuminated in the plane's winglights.

That hospital staff wouldn't know us.

That we will continue to fail to realise that people we love are dead.

That we will work with our mistakes until they look intended.

That chairs would not be stacked around us as though something more than closing time had begun.

That theorists would not become theories.

That we will not so often see in dreams adult versions of the kids we went to school with whom we haven't seen since.

That eclipses would make us think of something other than blindness.

That the horizon will not be mountains but sea.

That we would continue to mistake one face for another, but only briefly.

That passing runners would not cough on us.

That clouds would continue to surprise us with their three dimensions in spring.

That we would see again a kaleidoscope.

That there would be a declaration of the rights of feeling that wasn't *The Sorrows of Young Werther*.

That there would be a much earthier word for *frisson*.

That evidence stricken from the record would not remain more strongly in the mind.

That we will not answer *every* piece of correspondence in our correspondent's voice.

That it would not take a crisis to displace a crisis.

That spring sunlight would not be so eager to drag us out.

That Eden would continue to mean *too much of a good thing*.

That consciousness would not begin with the first lie.

That we could see (unassisted) Hamlet's total inability to love.

That the unsaid would not so often be kinder than the said.

That the fecund mind would not need to be cut in two.

That we will touch our face less.

That always we would know the owner.

That more motions would feel like swimming.

That we wouldn't judge anyone, ourselves included, on whether or not the soles of their shoes wear down lopsidedly.

That far more art would be as sustaining as gossip.

That *spontaneous* would not mean *badmannered*.

That we wouldn't prepare for the urologist as though for a date.

That we will not value anything in proportion to the number of words it engenders.

That snow, when collected in a pan then heated, would not reveal itself to be mostly dirt.

That cockroaches would not hide in and then jump out of coats.

That views would not have to contain humans in order to mean.

That we will never want to *take anyone with us*.

That the chief reason for our goodness would not be fear.

That we will never live in a house we love.

That integrity would be more than the desire to maintain the high opinion of oneself.

That *different from* would not so often mean *better than*.

That in memory we would understand firework displays.

That no one would be impressed by their own handwriting.

That we would again underline description, rather than rush through it.

That we would never see the written plans of the recently dead.

That we could again hear the world holding its breath on certain winter nights.

That we would never choose an empty train carriage.

That vacancy signs will never be turned off to save money.

That we would find a cafe in which we could sit all night.

That we would not find a cafe in which we could sit all night.

That we would not regret stopping to collect ourselves too soon.

That all honest diaristic writing would not in part be very irritating.

That companies will stop congratulating us.

That the choice would not be between poetry or doubt.

That death could lose *some* of its originality.

That what remains is not mostly what might have been.

That we would hear the organist practising in a deserted church.

That pain would become embarrassed by its repetitions.

That we would still see the trees moving slowly in the storm.

That darkness would not sharpen hearing.

That we wouldn't make links at the weakest points.

That real faith would not always bring with it the craving to have that faith tested.

That we would not come to awareness only in the transitions.

That silence would *never* answer.

That hell would remain visible only to those not in it.

That the only thing wrong with nostalgia would be its timing.

That there would be a nearby river in which to cool bottles.

That the only freedom would not be the *manner in which*.

That we could visit a church for some reason other than a funeral.

That we would not be so arrogant as to easily and often admit our mistakes.

That writing would be more than a way to convince the writer of having lived.

That not everything would be better enjoyed at one remove.

That *Jesus* would treat his mother more kindly.

That shared pain would not be the last defence against solipsism.

That we could quote a good line by a bad writer.

That when caught looking we wouldn't look away so quickly.

That birds would not need REM sleep.

That we wouldn't see so easily the child in the vicious adult.

That it would only ever come out of overabundance, rather than hunger.

That solitude will remain in ignorance of itself.

That no ditch would be the last.

That *every* ditch would be the last.

That most noses would be different.

That no rooms will need apologies for our having lived in them.

That suburban spring would continue to say, even as we laugh, *We have it in us to triumph over hate and death.*

That the ashes would be, at least, lucidity.

That we could remember the prayers we offer in our sleep.

That we would not bury *everything* that dies.

That we could have night's depth of feeling with morning's ability.

That those waiting to be asked would not vastly outnumber those capable of asking.

That there would always be someone watching.

That our mother would not so often be that someone.

That our mother would not be the one who watched first.

That children would not learn about the holy before they have any need of it.

That apathy would not be the only true panacea.

That music would continue to renew the old clichés.

That no one will label anything *puckish*.

That replying to messages will not become *too* easy.

That the Infernos in art would not so greatly outnumber the Paradises.

That *about to* would last much longer.

That the self and the prayer-self would at least occasionally be the same.

That *normal people* would not be only those we've just met.

That forgiveness would be far more difficult.

That we will stop having the dream in which we're shot in the head.

That we would've started rejecting a little later in life.

That we could imagine where the humans went when expelled from Eden.

That each failure would be different from the last.

That the dead would not be reduced to a state of *objecthood*.

That the black hole at the centre of Proust's work would not be the death of his mother.

That tears would never be only the idea of tears.

That we will not become our own concordance.

That the absence of belief in an afterlife would not allow us to shirk our duties to the dead.

That we would not have to sacrifice one half of ourselves in order to live completely with the other.

That Hopper would paint even just a single close-up.

That we'd remember the phrase *very pretty in a cold and blackhaired way*.

That no one would suffer the indignity of being a magician's assistant.

That Athena would not stop playing her pipe merely because it distorted her face.

That sunlight would not oppose imagination so violently.

That we would always be ready to fall to our knees.

That we would not fall to our knees.

That we would stop beginning sentences with *Years ago*.

That refusal would not be far more vainglorious than acceptance.

That someone would say *moonlorn night*.

That we won't disappear in the fog.

That the loss of the fear of death would not lead to the loss of feeling.

That we would not need to be miserable to enjoy bad films.

That a definition of *boring* would not be *saying everything*.

That as a kid Malte would not paint only islands.

That the elderly will sing in their hospital beds.

That we will never hear their singing.

That we will not outlive ourselves.

That we wouldn't always want to know the name of the sayer before the saying itself.

That no one would say goodbye from the platform as the train departs.

That thinking everyone dishonest would not be the surest way of becoming dishonest.

That memory would work as well outside of solitude.

That we would see beaches covered with snow.

That *never using anything up* really would be a saving grace of never finishing anything.

That clothes would not so easily fall to, and so easily remain on, the floor.

That nature would not be so keen to hide.

That we'd need never *execute* the plan (any plan).

That we will continue to have periods of such amorphous happiness that people think we're stupid.

That it would be possible to look away from a man struggling to untie his shoelaces.

That if we must address ourselves out loud, we'd use sentences of only one or two words.

That we will pour so as to fill.

That mystery would always find a home in a quiet street at dusk.

That childhood would stay put.

That the city will change more quickly than we – but not anyone – can map it.

That the innocent could prize innocence.

That we would not try to *make use* of everything.

That it would not take eight hours of free time to do two hours of work.

That poetry would not be the apotheosis of not-living.

That we will now and again see fish ripple by like a river in water.

That Horatio would not try to kill himself at Hamlet's dying.

That Schubert would see the sea.

That our mother would die only with us.

That the ages of the dead calculated as though still alive would continue to shock us.

That now and again we'd hear of someone out there looking for the literal Fountain of Youth.

That joking would have a purpose other than evasion.

That the sky's death throes would be less embracing.

That we will not get *too* adept at unhearing.

That our mother's being dead would not cause others embarrassment.

That we could know what the ostrich sees in the sand.

That humility would not be a disgrace.

That we will not measure weakness in others by the ways in which they grieve.

That every social occasion would be as enjoyable as a wake.

That moralists would have a greater sense of form.

That attention really would be the natural prayer of the soul.

That today would be as graspable as tomorrow.

That Odysseus would not mean *man of pain*.

That Odysseus *would* mean *man of pain*.

That inner and outer weather would never align.

That the poem would not be realer than the ruins.

That like fungus we could go through both doors at once.

That if we said *ribbit*, someone would say *ribbit* back.

That Yorick would not be the one whom Hamlet kisses most often.

That we could hear *Just Before Dark in the Forbidden City*.

That Socrates would not always want to prove the other person wrong.

That we will learn to not apologise.

That we will hear the piano through the windows, through the walls.

That we would never *see* the stupid metaphors of the flowers.

That primates would be as graceful, as unclumsy, as the other orders.

That Odysseus, despite his reputation as unrestrained, incautious, would be better remembered for his maniacal ability to *suppress* his desires.

That our hand would stop twitching.

That our arm would stop twitching.

That our leg would stop twitching.

That our foot would stop twitching.

That Mother's Day really would be the lowest-crime day of the year.

That photographs would not reproduce with such fidelity the appearance of the people in them.

That we will not in fear turn to the third-person.

That Yorick's being Hamlet's real father would be better known.

That the silence between songs would be filled by rain.

That we will arrive in the great city in the gold of its night.

That Baudelaire would not be so skully.

That mornings would be gratuitous.

That we would not resist film skies becoming our own.

That Socrates would not condemn his wife and kids to poverty and humiliation.

That Mass would not work only when delivered in a language we don't know.

That clouds filtering sun would continue to remind us of the smell of peaches.

That Odysseus would weep less.

That Odysseus would not weep less.

That everyone would be treated, but not act, like a guest.

That the end of contemplation really would be purity of heart.

That we will not take pleasure in houses falling into the sea.

That no one would remember exactly the origins of the injoke, but everyone would nevertheless now and again search for it.

That the future would return to being amorphous.

That we would remember the evenings when we saw it all.

That we would invent the mornings, the afternoons.

That Telemachus would not, even subconsciously, want Odysseus to've died.

That the rats would not have to go to work in snow.

That we will not walk around in one sock merely because we can't find the other one of the pair.

That rows of trees wouldn't make us think of monuments to the slain.

That candles would give only their small light.

That it will not always be *Song of the End, Song of the Beginning*.

That each page could not be the first page.

That the flowers we remember would continue to be only those in bloom.

That the light in *Gatsby* would not be, of all colours, *green*.

That we would not need woods to be the landscape's subconscious.

That the weight of things, as well as the numbers, would not be on the other side.

That in a far summer the monks will be playing football.

That remaining where you started would not be thought a failure.

That remaining where you started *would* be thought a failure.

That people would continue, however needlessly, to count the seconds between thunder and lightning and tell us how many miles away the lightning is.

That secret rulers would not be the most proud and implacable.

That we will not be afraid to sneeze.

That we will not feel awkwardly shaped pieces of furniture lodged in our head.

That we would not begin *everything* in medias res.

That we will not run out of faces.

That we would never have to *see* anyone singing the *Winterreise*, especially anyone in tails, especially anyone in tails standing beside a grand piano, holding it.

That newsreaders would now and again be unkempt.

That occasionally about being right we could be as certain as about being wrong.

That poetry will be flammable not only in sickness.

That we would not see again lived-in rooms newly bare.

That the words of saints uttered in bad faith would choke the speaker.

That we would not pretend that those who look upon hell have wonders to tell us.

That we could have just one *Walpurgisnacht*.

That self-love would not be the reason most souls end up in Dante's purgatory.

That the ability to stand nonchalantly on a snail would be considered a serious character defect.

That we will not forget that the secrets of Ancient Egypt were also a secret for the Ancient Egyptians.

That the obstacle would not forever replace the object.

That we would not have to pay the usual price to hear the chanting of the penguins.

That the hospital could be remembered as the hospital of our births.

That *no* would continue to be the wildest word in the language.

That Dickinson would agree to come down and see Emerson.

That Dickinson would *not* agree to come down and see Emerson.

That we would not believe so firmly in everyone's self-stories, including our own.

That we wouldn't put the stories ahead of the deeds.

That we wouldn't put the stories *in place of* the deeds.

That the nurses' concern would be feigned.

That the trees will never outgrow their fields.

That *something* could be thought through to the end.

That nothing could be thought through to the end.

That longing could be more than confession.

That no one will say *we hardly knew them*.

That we could take a midnight drive to Chartres.

That place would not always be buried under the present.

That in hospital the unmoaning would not scare us more than the moaning.

That someone will say *Heaven to talk as we did.*

That we will never forget we loved, even if only once.

That we will remember that our mother will never have cancer.

That we could not ignore a distant scream, even in the deepest country.

That it would not be so quiet afterwards.

That the buildings we grew up around would not now be so much smaller.

That we will be the glass shivering, rather than shattering, with its own ringing.

That our veins would stop collapsing.

That we will continue to feel the gap grow between words and reality.

That we will be those in whom god dreams.

That *nothing* will be defined by our attitude towards it in the months, weeks, days before death.

That Dickinson would see the sea.

That we would not want so strongly to listen in to those who talk to themselves.

That we would remember seeing from a train window smoke rising Grimmly behind distant trees.

That we could stay among the meanings we have taken so long to make.

That around hospital skies shades would not speak.

That no one would take decades to notice the scar on their mother's face.

That by begging it to stay it will go away.

That we would have time to form *old* friendships.

That we would be able to pronounce – but not need to pronounce – those names out of myths other than our own.

That we will see again lightning across an open field.

That we will not accidentally join a search party for ourselves.

That we will not know what anyone else is in for.

That we would not push the alarm instead of the flush.

That we would not *come to*, but *come from*.

That we would be wary of those who answer neatly.

That we will not be able to cry *We were!*

That our rooms will be, in the words of a detective, *in disarray as in messy, but not as in foul play.*

That light, instead of falling, and falling, would hand it all over to darkness in an instant.

That we won't be fooled into thinking the deathbed view's any truer.

That we could again have *the usual at the usual at the usual.*

That we would still see, in empty winter beaches at low tide, a time before us all.

That at the end *we* will be done.

Pray out your unrest

* 9 7 8 1 9 1 5 0 7 9 7 6 3 *